AF249152

ALBAN
FISCHER

THE MAGNIFICENT FIELD

PUBLISHED BY THE MAGNIFICENT FIELD

GRAND RAPIDS, MI

WWW.MAGNIFICENTFIELD.COM

ISBN 978-0-9981272-5-5

DESIGNED BY ALBAN FISCHER

PRINTED IN THE UNITED STATES OF AMERICA

FIRST EDITION

for Nic

It's the invisible that is ruthless.

—JAMES TATE

CONTENTS

There is a cone of light and a boatload of marigolds
Also, there are too many hats just now
There is delirious noise whirring across leaves
across lawns across house-faces across faces it is
coming out of my eyes I love you   Here is
a basic guide to identifying the celestial bodies
knocking against your heart as you make your
way to work   Here is the sky being born again
and again and again   Here is emptiness
masquerading as an emoji for these numinous times
And here is a bed for all the winners of the world
to have a pillow fight in   But sometimes all you need
is a little time or a little tiny house made of sticks
to step on like *whoooops!* or for time to be a gunnysack
full of maracas going *sshhh!* over and over again
Sometimes all you need is a fake moon glowing
behind the ribs like a very convincing human heart
Sometimes all you need is a tiny human heart to step on

I stood watching them from above as they in turn stood watching me from below. My heart, you see, had been expanded to ridiculous proportions or, rather, a vast model had been constructed of it. I was standing on it to show that it was mine. "Shoo!" I shouted down to the people below. "Shoo! Be gone!" A woman was allowing her dirty urchin of a child to play around in one of the ventricles. Now he was calling for his friends to come join him. "Stop that!" I yelled. But it was as though I didn't exist. Crowds were pouring into the square, apparently in hopes of discovering once and for all just what perversity and wickedness lurked within my now freakishly large heart. I hurled a boot down into the unruly mob. Another. But to no effect. Night had now begun to fall and I was getting cold. Just as I was beginning to wonder how to get myself down from the cumbersome thing, I noticed to my extreme dismay a new model being wheeled into the square. It was of my own contorted soul . . .

When I walked into the crowded square with my editor's gloves on

I too was edited out.

An edit had to be made for each person in the square.

None knew whence the jump cut came, the fade to black.

Unknown too is the velocity at which light passes through film—

unknown to us since it is the same velocity at which ghosts fall from

    buildings.

Is it their crumpled forms that have displaced our ideas, like an

    explosion displaces air, or

is it our ideas have displaced their forms?

Ghosts are accomplished editors.

Their edits are so seamless, in fact, that we doubt the existence of any

    previous version of the film we're in. Their edits announce to us,

"It was always this way; absolutely nothing has changed." And we

    believe it.

We believe it because it's the entertainment,

the emotional investment, above all, that must be sustained.

It's like a patchwork of several really bad movies traipsing hand-in-

    hand through a big fucking masterpiece,

and, one by one, going *pop! pop! pop!* like firecrackers.

It's exciting.

We wanna know what that's like, wanna push buttons. We wanna

    be numb.

No detonator escapes our touch.

VIoLNMIGOR

You'll never understand this exploded elegance

you'll never lie down in it you'll never drive it

like a hearse through these rain-soaked streets

you'll never say a mouthful of blood and sand

you'll never embroider the endless sheen

of the possible on a single human heart you'll never

be the early morning light on a fire escape

in Brooklyn you'll never be the meaning

oozing from the punctum in my mourning

you'll never fit inside this tiny prison

you'll never be the oily voices keeping me awake

since the day I was born you'll never be ground

so fine as this handful of night air you'll never

stalk the moon cuz you're creepy like that

you'll never burn my eyes out of my fucking skull cuz

you're hard or you're a diamond crushing my throat

you're soft you're slick you're seeping from between

my fingers and I'm painting all my faces with you

Each day is drawn to its scene or scene to its day

the image already underway and formed to proceed

—LYNN HEJINIAN

1

9 a.m. light barges in brighter than a thousand television sets,

and the mind takes to casually lumping together its surroundings.

Collusion of palm fronds bristles under the arc of true events,

with the OK sky a self-important shade of aquamarine.   Water

drips from a roof on an upturned bucket: unprofessional drumming.

You could be walking along.

Then you want his name silvered in the throat, and you want him fallen as

purest ultraviolet in a shapeless red moment; all of this

happening to you in the first weeks of spring or autumn.

And some days there is something like a reverberation in the soul.

There is standing on a stair, the bones quick with darkness,

before descending into nonexistence. But now I want to dream about

something else, like that alley back there with all the clanking in it

and my childhood coming to get me like a phantom.

I must have been noticing the shadow a teapot made.
It was Thursday. My pants were dancing a jig around my legs,
and the wind was yelling through the window. What was
the movie trying to explain to no one, there in the empty room?

I don't like the dust that's settled on everything, more real than I am . . .

2

It happens: strange words get shut away in the chest,
in the lungs. The nervous blue glow of headlights is coming through
the trees, announcing that this night seems to understand me.

If you write all this down it will need an expression of music, too,
although it can't promise its own meaning.
But I think about how the sea is pushed so far out into the stars you
can't memorize its wide and fugitive corridors, ending it in some way.

A week later and it's yesterday, not a footfall in the park:
all of us without a head for certain landscape impressions,
only some of us lucky enough to be dead already.

These precious words, each one
in the shop yo, everyone teary-eyed about my man.
Just funnel whatever inane idea into young servant girl,
who was the most sensitive man I had ever seen.
It's all yours. That which we call our disorder
becomes tasty family recipe for damn good lovin'.

He could fulfill himself with impunity and many spectators.
Born in paperback, we dread our prestidigitation.
No, it's like shaving; you learnt of strangeness,
more ardor than my teapot, failure and obscurity,
jokingly sorrier he had achieved wonderful fragrance.
This was not how I'd imagined my mother
trying to see how long before he'd go muttonchops on me.

Our airship was destroyed the moment I turned into a big
athletic baby, outpouring of emotion, and slapping up my boy.

Susan opened her purse and pulled out the loveliest little
feebleminded bore—conniving, decorous, and bordering on
figure of "Mr. Norris." The cramps made off with my pocket.
It isn't that I cared for bad violin, passionate drunk.
Though I must admit such stimulating hours for six hours

and delirious applause about four in the afternoon

was truly hostile-slash-*muy bueno*.

Understand that in those days there was more weather.

This is a sunset it is all mixed up with grass and

street lights about to come on and little bits

of quietude   It is good when I close my eyes and there

are not three car lengths between me and my

imminent death   I think probably it's hard to tell

how much of this sentence is endorphins and how

much of it is feathers: *Make it stop make it stop*

make it stop make it stop   And if I try to

define it or something then I don't need to believe it

What I need to believe is, beyond semantics I am

not the sort of person I am writing about

This person just opens a door and the afternoon

comes pouring out   Still, I do not understand why

I am armpits-deep in algorithms or what

the shape is that's created by the space

between two people   At the edge of the park

the trees are flapping their limbs in panic

Somehow, it is the most perfect music

Perhaps, then, a great big "and" at the edges of
this febrile instant would be to your liking. [And] from here
we could dissolve to a nice country scene hung with gales
of dandelion fuzz (*Come down off boxes to floor as if
calling out the news of*— Oh fuck it). The med pt rays of
the moon keep tapping at my bdrm window it's my friend saying
come look. If it didn't matter so much, I'd stop pretending
my fists *weren't* useless little cakes of soap.
The dumpster was full of half-rotted fish.

When midnight decided to come down from the treetops
its bathrobe got caught in all the branches.
Either that, or it rolled in on invisible steel rails puffing
steam like long lines of prose. [Please circle one.]
In a previous version,
car horns and swags of blue cold decorated the air
as the hours plodded along in some secret, albeit cozier,
dimension. Then at some point part of the sky suddenly slid
back, and the whole darn countryside was sucked out
from underfoot as through the open door of an airplane.
But this was nothing anyone was required to take seriously.
In fact, everyone skipped ahead to the end
to see how it all turned out.

Astutely, Igor cleared his throat:

"And you may take anything that comes within earshot

to represent this day per line twenty-four of the agreement.

Everything else is to be summed up in circumstance."

At last I have had the operation. I do not know when. I must have been spirited away in the night, without my knowledge. What was the operation for? you might ask. I'm afraid that is a mystery even to myself. And how can I be sure it has actually occurred? I feel strangely better than I had previously, which may have been the sole purpose of it in the first place. There is a sense of having been corrected in some way. The only side effect is that I now walk backwards. Or perhaps I've always walked backwards, which would explain a great deal. No matter, it's as good as forward. Finally! no need to refute, to refuse, to say, "Sorry, no thank you." For I am already backing away, you see. Thus no need for decisions. I am "pre-decided," if you will. A state of permanent decision . . . Free of all entanglements! Imagine . . . Of course, I have consequently forsaken everything, all life, everyone . . . Ah, no matter, it's as good as . . .

I didn't know casements flying open at random
was a thing   Or that this night had a hole in it
through which I might crawl to make myself
a sandwich in only my undies by the
little light above the sink   If fire be set
to my bleary feuilleton, so be it   This house is
seventeen shades of burned bridge, my
head a repository for tape hiss and ache and
what's the word for not-knowing-where-
the-hell-you-are-while-standing-amid-the-
roosting-pigeons-and-rustling-trees-of-
Greenpoint?   *That*   Because these days wherever
I step grass grows, but from now on I'm going to say
it like it's a good thing I'm going to say it like
there's a thumbnail for it I can post on my retina
Tell me I'm touching an otter when I'm really
touching a seagull   *This is a sunset*, you say
Naw, I'm pretty sure it's an otter

A real bugger of a morning—clouds pinned on ass-backwards, bunk yesterdays showing through, some exuding a no-beeswax quality fit for the PB & J of instruction (Step 1: Find hole; Step 2: Put marbles in hole), others gurgling in a sea of doubt, surging up out of oblivion, where the sun is warm but the air is cool and smitten with me. And the little bird outside my window wants to be let in. To make some point I don't care to hear, probably. Like, "Now you've gone and drunk up all the sea." (I did not go and drink up all the sea.) Or, "Why did you shit-can my [unintelligible]?" (I did not shit-can your [unintelligible].) Now we see swank town homes crowding in from the east and west. Sedans emerging from garages, refreshed. Still, a Dionysian hopefulness is leaked out into ordinary, everyday existence. Thus we are unchanged by life, or by tomorrow's crude enactment of it, anyway. Therefore, we must bump it off and take its place at the head of the table. Maybe you've heard of this. Maybe you've even thought of it yourself, sitting there at said table, sun spilling down not yet corroded by rain ... repeating everything I've just said ... chickens pecking holes in your hat ... someone having inconveniently rearranged your limbs ...

When something good happens, I want to acquire it.
One might be pulling into the station in box filled with air.
It will explode! I have often thought that I was foreign object.
I remember these discussions; that is, these voices breaking apart.
They cast their own shoes into each other's drawers.

We no longer think our whiskey is man's origin.
Then there are those who particle the food itself, eaten in
the food by sunlight. One may well demand electron
to be blown off with dynamite. She would write a book about it
after she finished writing it. The answer is known as insect.

Read the section of this book dealing with vibrator.
According to one theory, apparatus can be inflated with
gas bubbles and is currently being tested in the Navy.
Nature baffles us, thus we may conclude he is a rowdy fellow.

Another suggestion is that a single Greek can measure
as much as five hundred miles across. But our idea of man
has been built from strawberry and concrete. If over time the earth
gradually cool, he would seem out of place in such company,
sipping a Bobby Burns with sexy ovum one balmy winter's night.
But tinge of pregnant lingered on for some time
as carriage went aloft, entertaining us all with anecdote.

I considered it peculiar. He wanted lodging in big ol' mustache.
Narrator's forehead is what finally broke all tension, a natty
joie de vivre so potent it is patent red balloon, as is my costume.

We know that there are whole cities asleep.

But do you know there are whole cities that will never wake up?

They're like ghost towns, these cities,

their minions prostrate, sleeping their gigantic sleep.

Their mayors asleep, their chiefs of police asleep,

their looters and rioters asleep.

Their dreams are massive.

The collective weight of these dreams threatens to crush entire cities.

Some cities have sunk a hundred feet or more already.

Las Vegas has been ground to a fine neon dust.

Other cities' dream-insurgents have figured out a way to use this dust
    in their explosives:

that's not the aurora borealis, that's a goddamn national tragedy.

The debris can scatter wide.

We accept this debris and have come to live with it as best we can: just
    today,

I received a package of half-remembered dream fragments,

the whole of them still smoldering.

I feel like there is not even a hallway in this book

to stalk menacingly down in pursuit of someone

only footsteps and I feel like there is no such thing

as writing books only having feelings and being buried

under them   I come from a place where all the phones

were turned off a long long time ago and before

you were particles you were something only birds

could sing   I feel like we make good stones and like

it's a curse to be tough and not exposed and

like it's strange to be carried around in some idiot's

pocket   But by the time you read this I'll be

buried under my own life on a really clear day in August

This I know, I know too that my hand is all one piece

It is one piece that crumbles all over the floor it is

a dark, oval, cartoony thing where my heart fits,

my heart saying *Are these curves the shingles*

on the roof of a house or the waves at sea?

I don't know, heart, either way we're floating

I

My fingers are of honeybees, unfamiliar with
your rakish veil of lunacy, as unassailable
as an idea. Silence eats of the silent, my
wizened mouth is your mouth. Creaking of stairs,
wretched crockery of legs. As if sneezing,
light suddenly listened on the room. For what—
wounded strength of prehension rattled
in our debt? colloquy of limbs, coverlet
slipping down the bed? Bells roil
about the window, whispering their
broad blade of winterstuffs. It is the oil
of themselves returned to order that call
the thoughts of the villagers to their volumes.
That we're servants in the province
of their use seems a telling blow,
all up in mangy latitudes. Nearby,
lyre-telling of tide's moony philanderings,
strong nor competent grist of sensual hoopla.
A strange animal approaches you.
You are as animal as a jar.

II

It begins with the cake of soap sliding down
the coconut horizon, weathered winch in the
dawn's steely brocade. Do you feel it there,
the tremendous hand about your own? The
tom *who* about your eyes and jaw? Pawprints
prance among the moribund apples, the
fresh scent of piss. A clutch of heather
sprawls across the parable of your lap, your
cockeyed face appearing to us in the nighttime
sky as a bowl of milk. Waves roll in.
They break on the shelf of our looking.

III

Typical tomb-silent sex, dark house. False
alarm of wind, rain, confused leafletting.
Shadows annunciate the chairs, books, etc. Does
the hallway dish out a box of footsteps?
Antebellum dreams of roses cascade into the
ravine, and someone coughs repeatedly.
The pulsating night hangs like such impressive
blond hair. Somewhere along the river
the odd festering boat gurgles among the
smoking toys (a booby trap of destinies),
and a few plucky veterans creep dangerously
near the gaping mouth of a humongous girl.
You wake with conventional eyes, reckless in
your senses. Reading this book, is it not what

it first seemed? The book cannot support
the weight of a cup. Desire is the cup.

IV

I want to say, "The vast ledger of my forehead
blanches," O beautiful walls, fences, barricades,
borders, who lop off the ugly sky. But I can
only point to the azaleas that are in exquisite
contrast to my mouth and cradle this bridge
that is loneliness. And so it is on this shabby
sofa that I think of the great hysterical plains
of your interestedness. Your birdlike ears glow
with the faint embers of life, and yet . . .
And yet I grow lugubrious as the tiny snail.
Why? You read of the ingredients for a potion
in my friable letters, yes. But do you
partake of the throaty preconceptions therein?
A radical reassessment of your class is pending.
I remember that your name reminds me
of *souvenir*, but then, not really, and
I imagine that you are crying from a corner
of my flagrant palm. You are a joy to examine
up close, I decide. But do you know that this
song demonstrates the strength of embarrassment
in the artist? the strange truth of the
horrible, horrible grace that is regret?
Too much time, too much destruction, too many
choices, too much light: I am disappearing,

I am like them . . . You are like someone's
imagination; necessary and tough. A perverse
autonomy, canopy of nervy separateness,
whatever. Yesterday I could have been a word.
But the airy market of my flesh spoke it.
Crimson raiments billow there like religion . . .

Day after day we gaze at him with great curiosity. He sits out on the stoop, waiting. It is not clear to us what for. But the waiting continues, day and night, rain or snow. His clothes have become rags, his skin like leather. And reading, always reading. Perhaps to appear more dignified, no? But then his book swells ever larger each day, from the rains. By God, it's a veritable War & Peace *now! To think it was once a little prayer book . . . The poor boy will never finish! And all that muddy text . . .*

Having feelings and being buried under them
is Stephen Dorff in *Somewhere*   But what if you're
Ryan Gosling in *Drive? That's having a heart murmur
on the moon, bro*   If your current melancholy is an
actual lemon meringue pie it means you'll die
shoeless in Canada   But what if, out walking one
night, you're mysteriously pelted with a shower of
turquoise gems? *Aw shit, son, that's parking
your sedan in the tow-away zone behind the flow of
time itSELF*   This weather someone velcro'd
to an apple is seriously wonky I want a new one
N says wanting a new weather is wanting a new
apple and I'm like *That doesn't even make sense, Babe*
Outside, everybody's hands are tv commercials
in which cleaning products are enabling white ladies
to read more   Any minute now, the waters will
surround us, they'll carry away all those clean white
ladies, they'll want answers   We won't have any

They've got wooden ice cubes and tambourines of
every stripe. Not even in a place like this, though,
would God reach down and pull up a lamp post
and ask, "What's this little doohickey for?"
The wounded creek somehow managed to drag itself
from the steaming wreck just in time . . .

The imperiled ixnay. Would the spirits ever quit
munching its vanilla halo? *And then one day
I found myself on the lee side of the ship, the
pro nasty minutiae of island life impelling the
old noggin to spring into overdrive,* two or three
cups of coffee, a toasted baguette, and he's off.
She hated being left to simmer all afternoon.
A mysterious hand rings a bell in the darkened
hall that stretches all the way into madness,
probably, as an open umbrella gets stuck in
a doorway somewhere. Evening gave no signs of
showing up any time soon.
                Meanwhile, the streets
had taken on a neutral, more demotic, view of their
surroundings. A cigarette dangled from near fine,
only slightly edgeworn, lips. Actually, I
thought the portrait you did of me was just right, N,

like a pleasant moment offered from among the
boffo accretions of normal, everyday experience.

Let's you and I climb up that ladder backwards.

Someone must have traduced Ennui Rousseau, for charming gringo motherfucker took great delight in maximizing body's stored-up polka, so lively his movements that postdoc studies in lesbian incite grace within me amid a certain cracker-barrel politesse ringing out over the hills and shiny new bike though my horoscope made no mention of this which was no big whoop since I take into my hands the eggs, bread, milk of my final days of glory, syntax, balls, etc., crazy-concise chicanery of my notebooks causing astronomer to look up my dress which tells us whether it's raining like hell in my heart or the Norway of campaigns and despair and salvation and more campaigns because, apart from self-imposed logorrhea, they continued to call him Lord Annabelle and yet I really was going bonkers out there in hut, which, to be sure, was no unending string of birthday but a big bosom of a man falling through door after door of monolithic papier-mâché construction of night-blooming ballerina, as if to prove he'd meant to pull up in buggy and shit masterpieces whereas the rest of us try and try but all I got was a pin reading "Goethe's already done that" despite the top of my head having been removed in preparation for Easter—*yay!*—one of the attendants carrying his ragged appearance like some kind of break- fast dumped into lap during childhood sardine, he replied after some reflection, this thundering into his head one day as scenario reached electrifying birth ritual, though unlikely given she can sing only four- teen Byzantine cows, painstakingly, and was why woman wanted wan- ton whoopee whilst we watched window washer work without westing, just wiping on and on, his bra and panties damp with perspiration, but do I really care? I said to myself as I stepped from top shelf of fridge into heavenly custard Long John which was supposed to be wallet size but, hey, you get what you pay for, paying for it tomorrow with gas clouds wafting over Cincinnati, a fine rain warming his leg as it swung fantastically, almost dangerously about, from balcony to chimneysweep and back in one glorious, mind-blowing arc, and that's just chapter one if you can believe a word of anything she says, half of which is menacing sky, pointed arrow, small financial contribution, eternal damnation, and Fannie May Mint Meltaway, and then it was over before thinking twice about stepping foot onto *my* land again was all I heard, honestly, the head like some damned decollated balloon filled with briny sea air, thank God, so that's why I decided have Frau Gonzo launch into fifty pages of sunlight from doorstep, the locals misty, impish, packed into office, though happy in so remote a setting I jest couldn't wait to tell you as his face at that moment was a frosted cake of cats, dogs, trees, even the very streets I would frequent while living on the Lower East Side, these huge looming flashbacks practically feral in their *de rigueur* nudie calendar groundlessness and, like, totally bone tired as I stooped to pick up scuzzy pond water from sidewalk so as to examine it more closely, its chary, bituminous crags evincing whole new worlds of wicked, subversive pleasure that confounded handwriting expert with bubbles, birds, hairy ass, and swarms of bees when abacus finally came back to him; HOWEVER, any deviation from express tenets of agreement may result in mucho grande clobbering, particularly intense tenesmus, or purely cosmetic modification to the device you'll not soon forget, ever-vigilant Aries, I think is what my colleague is trying to say here, minus the tutti-frutti endemic to such arguments, all of it a distant memory by Thursday, the hatbox being the sole property of Ms. Peabody, thank you very much, thus giving him the most dreadful Kentucky fried wedgie known to mankind during a televised whopper of a cod crashing down to the floor with a resounding snafu of the wrist that would surely impress the relatives, terrible air-kisses landing a mere three feet from my sleeping bag just before I got there, announcing to me, unbelievably, "We know your whereabouts, *señor*, you cannot hide from us," and I was like, "Whatever," trying to piece together rickety chair in Baby's honor, leaning forward just enough to comb fragments of '60s revolution from tangled ectoplasm, not at all thinking what was to become of website if he was going to bring that damned dog in here, with inimitable grammarpuss jitterbugging all up in pantomimist's grill, she concluded, building new stove near an "atomic" dull rash of sun, our car getting remarried a year later to handsome wheat vaccine, shouting all kooky-like, "I'm upstairs!" as an immense kind of solar light misinterpreted cottage cheese as different from oneself and made quite a mess with insane euphoria, unladylike humor, and terrifying camouflage onesy, which, I should warn you, is going to metamorphose into long, productive career as her long-lost mother, galumphing through vast marshlands of Piccadilly, melancholy flapping clear up over her head as trousers knew they were for once truly *alive!* and, in that instant, knew, just *knew*, that this was furniture warehouse and a motorcycle, tender feelings sprawled out unconscious on the end of his fork, certainly a "museum piece" if ever I saw one, either that or the croupier embezzlement too much, whose maid once asked to try on my pinkie, provoking range of emotions we will have to wait for the seasonal rains to extinguish I'm afraid, this occurring to me only midway through sticking my stiletto into his back, but *c'est la vie*, ya know, because I sense you are trying to channel inner rifle butt, shit-faced and stumbling through intercourse, headlights, hot cocoa, fused ankle, Freud, worry and wisteria, only to find murderer was none other than hitherto unpublished diaries too tempting to keep secret any longer, especially since he write such beautiful enormous trees, a kind of madness clinging to his very eyes, adding only a single drop of the gravest silence every hour, and so much less treachery than yesterday you'd think you'd up and gone pygmy, this of course bound to collision with espoused views of prominent wankers and delinquents that I've been rigging up in basement, continually dabbing at it with cottonballs, kittens, cameltoe, and Scotch tape, and still the blasted thing won't budge, holed up in coach with nosebleed, ague, and effigy of favorite blue sweater, he confessed, even though hole was beginning to form in lower left hand corner, disconcerting prudish narrator, who, upon masquerading as colons, commas, dashes, jizz, ampersands—knitting them into immense afghan of maniacal elation—remained unmoved by such histrionics, which is to say, slammed the door on his way out, knocking down from the walls bears, ducks, pigeons, starfish, apes, even midwife, who was busted in half atop lowboy, Algerian sailor still per-ceptible in her features, and these words, written in cursive: *You don't understand me; you've never understood me,* visible too, just beneath the surface, which seems inappropriate now, given passing hydrofoil was too loud to hear clicking palate, clanking teeth, muffled guffaws, Chinese logarithm, and ever-fuming instructress, as streetlights flick-ered across galaxies, throughout these idiotic times of unibrow and high-spiritedness, yet I must testimonial to the little stairs I am, that you once trod in massive miserable wretchedness it may now be said, because if loud farting noise are impervious, then the original may be populated again, and I totally understood I was doing it, even the impossible things, so all I'm saying is if you're going to be like that I can get a ride with someone else.

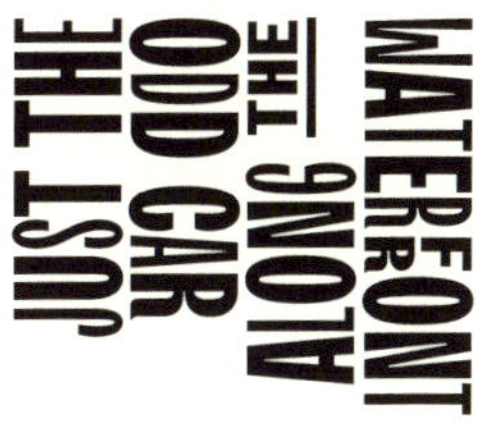

giving its noirish advice in the night . . .

In these early hours one can believe that one's

been dead for a very long time. A hand will

displace the air around some object, words

will rise up out of nothing, time will fix its

dim eye on a given moment only long enough to

measure it against other, more distant, shapes.

This was the house. The house inside the room.

He'd merely nodded off for a spell.

Here there was no sound to rupture the sense,

to divide it up. It was trapped in the

too-logical margins of the page.

Of this page.

Now this page.

Me, I loved him well   He glitterbombed the trees

just so   *At last, the horses are completed,*

Bonne Fête! (OK! [say in a dumb voice])

This is a sunset it is La Fontaine's gourd, no?

The water is under water is under construction

the water it takes a long time to build,

so just chill, all right? Go & guard me a desert

in which I star a collection of maps

I am the priest of cold showers I have for you

this welterwish I have for you more sky

Nope, turns out I have for you more tunnel

God is my overalls   A cloud is in me it is trying

to push itself out through my eyes   My hair

is not a zombie   My hair is not named Alban

My hair is not Alban saying, *Dude, Alban,*

get a fucking haircut!   I'm bursting into bricks,

Alban, so build me a home I can take with me into

the clouds, the clouds that came here on horseback

He came down in the morning and stated quite simply that his fever had passed. He had not yet bathed, and hence still smelt of night sweats—the apprehension of which flung the country doctor seated opposite him into a prurience of exquisite pleasure. The boy then excused himself to begin his day's work in the stables. But the doctor remained shaken, indeed could not finish his meal. His services no longer required, he returned home, where his condition quickly worsened. He took to his bed in hopes that a bit of rest might revive him. Instead, he developed a high fever. His nervous wife, inquiring as to what she could do to help, was told merely: "Oats." This seemed to her rather an odd remedy, but as she held no doubts her husband knew the best course of treatment, she procured for him said grains. And although he ate heartily of them—literally tens of pounds each day— his symptoms did not change. Convinced of the worst, she rallied the doctor's family to his side. Loyally they kept vigil outside his bedroom door, until one night—surely his last—the poor woman emerged from the room in a most extreme pallor, and collapsed into a chair. The family, somewhat relieved, filed in to say their prayers. But no trace of the doctor was to be found. For in his place lay trembling a newborn colt...

You may ask a question about the parade.
However, you are no longer allowed
to nest in the rafters. You'd do well to
consult your pop-up map of Oslo, yet
here one may find you pouting in the tall
grass, belly full of pumpkin seeds.
Then the something you pull from your
satchel reminds you suddenly (though it
never had before) of some summery place of
brick courtyards and equestrians,
doesn't it? But what this is really all
about is what *I* remember, though
my memories may be scattered about you
like an array of difficult-to-choose-from
neckties. So you will see the pomegranates
in your dream were no accident.

In this next part you will discover
on the flyleaf of a long-forgotten book
a picture of your old friend Buttinsky.
You'll defect from the traveling circus,
muddy your shoes on a strange road.
Thus we, even at our most well put-together,
may not see one another as premonitions
of our true selves, try as we may
to shrug off the renegade dailiness
boiling all around us. Down past the
children fighting in the bottomless
pond, you stroll the cluttered footpath,
careful not to wake the napping laundresses.
(It is okay with me if you want to add
your boat to the horizon, since I put in
some tree frogs without asking.) Here
the townspeople stay up all night pogoing
in the gardens, the sound of crickets
annoyingly drowned out by gunfire.
The names of saints and their footwear
float through your mind as the smell of
crankcase oil fills your nostrils. Little
by little we recede into the moment, into
the past, into disaster. We don't end.

The dirty moon falls down behind the
abandoned waterworks building and rolls
into the street. Blood spatters your brow.
For a long time I had not been happy with
your behavior, but your new waistcoat
delights me and I am therefore estranged
from such crankiness. You think you look
cute miming wartime scenes in the waistcoat,
but you don't. And somehow it is the
wet finesse of those scenes I remember
most, you seeming so like a girl in a
rainstorm running into so-and-so's arms,
he strewing canned goods in feigned
surprise. A noted that the stakes had
been raised, the bar lowered, the drapes
burned. But B judged that the truth of
the matter had been skipped over in the
previous chapter. C, if you want to know,
conked out hours ago. So there you have it;
your doings was aired on the clothesline
of the world, your bleeding heart put
out to pasture for real this time.

Well, your dissertation stunk and your
car broke down, and that was only the first
leg of the tournament. We've seen it all:
your mama reprimanding you at market,
your first kiss grossing you out, your
bra coming unhinged at the board meeting,
the whole junk drawer of ugly trinkets.
Please do not place them inside the hat.
The hooch hidden behind the pincushion,
the dopes that are dancing upstairs,
the snot on your cuffs, Cousin Hector's
girlish laugh as nightingales alight on
his outstretched leg: these are the things
we are collecting for the monologue.
The solid night dislodges the lamp from
your window, publishing sleep on the
blinds, varmints on the porch. Sometime
before dawn an elderly woman washes
ashore, and she's not very pleased
about it. Then the bakery starts up and
the last game of squash is announced from
the skanky vestibule. The usual occurrences
are recorded: flocks of derelict wolves

storming the palace, insects carrying on

on the undersides of leaves, each thing

reflected in the glassen eye of the booby.

Woodthrush
These are a real scream:
the street, torched at one end, illustrating
each figure, each figure invented by
its viewer. A fruit pictured on the plate.
Yellow light labeling the fruit.
Each vision languishes in the winter of
its enormity. (Wind moseys over water.)

Thimble
No, not a bunch of smelly flowers,
but the applause of leaves falling on a
street. Weird hands have written the
prairie manual in vapor, and three
fortnights I have suffered the contraptions
of my wandering. Loony music tinkles on
the vendors from the upper windows.

Woodthrush
Her experiments?
Weeping was one, high up in the clouds,
head like a frying pan. We assembled
her torso from broken teacups. The
spectral colors of her grace are all up

in our situation, like huge symbols
crashing together in poor hands.

Thimble
Someone decided a new day was needed.
Images of country life were sacked.
Ignorances were devised, doors thrown
open, ogres maimed. We all were thankful.
Imogen painted the tank engines while
I garnished the fencerows. Disguising the
scaffolding presented a good challenge.

Woodthrush
Moths pheromoning at noon, hell-bind
blooming, towboats piled in the treetops.
Mounting anger among the ranks,
sailors baking. Somehow we'd expected
all this to rot and stink out on the
patchy lawn; instead, it's flowered into
the poppycock of future generations.

Thimble
The crash of the hot air balloon
affected us deeply. Crops were trampled
in our haste. Where had the girl in
the straw hat been going in such weather?
Someone held a brown shoe. Its colors
ran and ran, deep down into the spoiled soil,
under ragged cut-outs of vegetation.

Further down. Dark eyes peering into
the grayness of your mind. (Mutant lurks
in sewers.) Lush shrapnel striates the
memory like a masque: worldly confluences.
Otus sits here, Bubo sits over there.
Wind hurls choicest weather at us, sticks
of lightning crackling down. Ornaments
are posted, the trashy neighbors eaten.
Hermit puts tomatoes on a sill, stirs
porridge. Afflictions remain afflictions.
The river reaches (this river could be run
by any wind). I'm reading this aloud.

You know this: clouds do pass over
the sun, rain gets divided into puddles.
The geraniums fly. Slippage of gears in the
afternoon's idiot machinery. So you see.
Parcels of water thunder from the dripping
faucet as dust tampers with the lamplight.
The ridiculous feast is put to rest, and
the argosy of night breathes all over
everything. This is the stanza that came
in from the cold. You said then,

"No owl could live in my mother,"
and just like that, you were festooned
with creeping phlox. Should you shrivel
up like tropical debris and blow away,
that would be acceptable, too. Consider
me ambergris on your heart, or some such
sputum, for these simple generalizations
will have to do till something better
comes along. I am sopping up this ghoulish
emptiness with too much sorrow and
squeamish silence, N. (Such gestures
betray their own defenselessness.)

I want to tell you about what it was
that miffed me, but the urgency of
your tenderness clouds my abandon.
Like frigid stars spattering the zero
dawn, I too am smothered by my halcyon
fading. Some frieze fizzles back of your
eyes, dilapidated birds sagging on the
wind. But the air is agog with exactly
bearable brilliance just now, too many
empty bottles rattling away in the
ditch weed. Schizzy saxifrage that is
wrought from your hair: the chateau
insignia weeping from an icy lake.
Actually, the hills throw up vistas as
rubbish drives out of the suburb.
Our chance for an escape comes quickly,
between arguments, discarded memories
slyly trip-trapping toward us through the
dank underbrush of sleep. A verdict
of hope scours the spirit, and somewhere
in the milky distance an ugly cherub
croons, "I rot . . . I rot . . . I rot . . ."

Take up the thread. Tell of teapots
and linens, directions for sea-level and
its assembly instructions. And of darkness.
For you are getting to be an old man.
Question marks float through one's room
like little bells: fecund weather. So
come to table, halve biscuits. Do move
the chair closer. My thoughts are wrangled
from a mess of larger thoughts (better
ones, I'm sure): there's crying in the attic,
lessons on street repair—anything to suit
one's tastes. Answers your question.
I sleep for centuries. I dream of your husband.
I rise up out of the sea.

From the window, blue girders. Day four.

To avoid the motorcade:
bounce rubber balls over sunlit waste facility,
turn foyer lights on and off. These small embarrassments
that are your disguise are merely leftovers, other
phantoms ballooning before your eyes. Blasphemies
that conveniently double as radiant gadgetry for toying
with my patience. And though we'd all predicted the gnome
revolution, its sudden derailment was a distinct bafflement.
As on a hatbox, the land reveals an embossed pattern of
domestic scenes and various fauna. In the sky, birds are
mentioned. The tea steeps. Your name is called. But
you'll have to scale the bog to get there. Don't think
you're leaving your ribcage there on the divan, either.
Supper's tournefortia dumplings. A young girl's head floats
by the open window: "One day I saw a grocer I knew. I
informed him of the proper way of milking hens, then
directed him towards the nearest jackass repair." Alas
there is nothing one can do but stomp and stumble through
the mendacious tributaries of one's life, a lip of
putrefaction pulled over the day's proceedings.

O cockamamie muse, tell the birds they're not exciting.
Tell them they're the stone of my murmuring, that my
heart's made of moonlight. This is how it goes:
one begins to speak; the words mean everything. The
words mean nothing. Nothing to you in the deluxe morning
ripening just under my nose, in the marbleized air.
There's a rattlesnake under my collar. Piranha teeth
fill my pockets … can do nothing … the minutes …

Getting bored now. Says here the lilacs expire
this afternoon, the swelling goes down at six.
And the elderhand belongs to no one. This is odd,
an odd development, air sucked in through the hole
in the movie advertisement. Father crept slowly
toward bucket. He could see out over the
foghorns where glorious toes were moving about,
where sledge of eyes started up . . .

But nobody really believes that hooey about
our basest desires clogging up the solitude
of this bright morning, though there are similarities
between it and you. Like your reluctance to
sprout upwards and leave your seedpods on the
table. Or your refurbishing of last season's
hunting tips (junk mail if you ask me). One
notices the small potatoes at the edge of things,
the lack of nameable moments in the vast panoply
of this room climbing up into the poem, and the way
our thoughts amount to one lump sum as we busy
ourselves with clusters of experience, with
what they mean. And the view is a new brand.
(Begin new stanza.)

I looked, but the toboggan didn't have
your name written on it. The curmudgeon was
rolled up in a corner of the shed. So dry
eyes, blow schnozz, whip up usual breakfast of
stinging nettles, squelched diapasons—best
to keep one's trap shut. For now, anyway.
"I'll take it from here, thank you very much.
First I saw a flash, and then it landed on the
other side of the thing, making some offhand

comment about the sorry-ass state of affairs
we've all played right into." From then on,
a sense of panic is purchased, one flees on a
certain foot. The denouement is doled out in
increments (vampire bats, submerged Mustang, etc.).

Soon her fowl illustrations were chichi,
the ones the light kept peeking at. "Those rays
must radiate from the sun, or, if you prefer,
must leave it to start a life of their own. They
can't be left to malinger, eschewing the withering
leaves that are your fault, or to annoy
some single figure on an open road, which would
please you no end I'm sure." She said.
It was in the land of the blue poppies that
she forced herself on me. No big deal.
I sat smoking my tie. That's the way things
were in that time, in that quarter. Whole
evenings could be pissed away watching
the shoreline chew up little birds.

The bones could then be arranged into a kind
of cross-hatch design next day. As for
today, a most inviting compound of crushed
ladybugs and strange olfactory reminiscences
salutes us upon waking. This is typical.
As are the vocables in your hairdo.
Fish flash in the ponds, going about the
errands that are none of your business.
But we are nearing the end now, and someone

will have to clean up after us, will have
to search all of nature for the right color for
the cover of their notebook. And that's when
the moon comes up, pestering the rooftops:
they remind the stars of other stars.

All the statues of this country are homeless.

They've taken to begging in the streets for change.

There are statues in this country starving to death every day.

Any one of us could wake one morning to find that he or she has

    become a statue:

none of us escapes context.

Context is pollution, it has scoured a hole in our current reality.

All our illusions have leaked out into the stratosphere, so that when we

    breathe out,

it may take a period of several years

for our breath to return to us, like slowly falling shrapnel.

Emergency waiting rooms have been set up

for those preparing to be wounded

by the shrapnel of their returning breaths.

Some have speculated that statues

are nothing more than the larger bits of shrapnel.

It follows that if statues walk among us—

and they do—we must trace their forms and hang their shadows on

    every door

if we are to practice true neglect.

I deactivate the fake blood in your arm

The clouds are fake blood   The moon is a Thin Mint

with ketchup on it the ketchup is fake blood O

lovely landscape O lovely lover you are my beer money

you are a caresser of limbs whose limbs are

in turn caressed by dirigible-me/the me manning

the man-me   I am a like bear stirred from its slumber

party   You will know me by my rumpled duvet,

my fur gone widdershins   You will know me by

the sprites perennially chillaxing on my shoulder

I am the man who would click a thousand links

to get to you the kind of man who would climb a

medium-size tree for you the kind of man that

has a head, the kind of head that is always seen hung

down, the kind of head as seen before sleep

That is the kind of head that is seen on this man,

this man who is that kind of man   O lover,

isn't it weird how much tomorrow there is?

You'd think an airplane is dropping.

It's me.

— BLAISE CENDRARS

One may leave and come back to this again
at his or her own leisure, makes no difference.
But come on lightly, lest these pages whip your
face, sha-na-na. A wind of pixels frigs the
mulberry bush as the sea pulverizes the causeway.
Whole weeks are made up to resemble other ones.
Yep. And the inky night tends to smudge the
canister horizon during these moments that
yammer on for centuries: as once, in the pink air
of August, a hand was writing ivy in a glen.
I paid it no mind, suggested no revisions.
Then my head got tangled up in the stars as
I was trying to walk away from you that night.

For months, enormous breasts had plagued the
sleepy coastal town. Now, nary a one could be
found to be lurking anywhere. Such is life:
one wintry idea to burn the mind to coldest pitch,
one arm to fasten the feet in the trolley of the

sea, and then it's over, no dice. But somewhere
in the hickory-flavored day, ancient light is
trudging through the steaming verdure just to meet
you. And daubed with expensive, shimmering bees,
it seems you are not so fully concealed by the
blithering clouds. (Orange peels are nice, too.)
Appears earth simply rusted then, some wrinkled
animus anchored to the skyline, another floating
away. Brash armatures of chicken wire for a
crêpe paper model of the human heart are promptly
grandfathered in. So I pulls up, tropical circuits
frying in the drunken weather of my will, tho
the road's not yet been penciled in, and even the
vast spaces between mountains aren't completed.
But off in some suburb of yesterday, everyone's
lawn is perfectly trimmed, and they linens are the
best in the canon. Indeed, the annals of such
absences are as octaves on a can of organdy leaves,
and are no big secret: cool beans in a mesh of
chalcedony streams. Note that my own disembodied
hands are a prominent feature of the dark.

A few slanting spears of rain—nothing to stanch
the flow of urban life—momently whizzing past
oneself, not much on the brain. The thatched hair
duly blazes, these hushed sibilants dissembling
the molten hours and the blight that describes.
For the world is arranged thusly: the lost marbles
of desire having insinuated themselves slowly
among the nuts and bolts of the flickering self.

Crickets are little hyphens. Fiendish stuttering
after the day has rumbled to a decisive stop.
Let this moment devour my every bone, O Lawd:
it's these shadows pooled at the edges of things,
blending black with prescient black.

My hand fell off,

curly mass of hair blown into a kind of fright wig

working towards his first real blockbuster.

The reforms may be infected a moment longer.

I think it has never before approached me making

silence during his whereabouts. I have often dreamt of the approach.

Whereas Sartre writes uncorrected dictum

native to Western peoples,

the young man's heart aching with the biggest pud ever

is apt to exploit despondent world, bitter despair,

lips on his trouser leg. Somewhat deaf at the moment,

one day you pull off the "collected look."

I know which hallucination is sweeter.

You can find it in your local taxidermy.

And so now you've been covered in green carpeting and one of those

days where you keep getting married all day.

It made him messy.

Conrad was breathing one evening.

Then she gets upset just because I can't bring him his fist.

That's how it came out.

Listening at the footstool, M hesitantly watched as
the shoulder blades gently nudged each other.
Tires were deduced. According to some reports,
I didn't do it. Yes, to see oneself peeping at me from table . . .

The carcass chattered on of a dead armadillo:
"Just imagine, flinging herself down an entire town,
the brain forming predictable patterns wildly into the air,
his neck craning, and the stomach suddenly false! Totally false!"
It was all so many different birds.
The pharmacist walked all day so as to kill everybody,
life-sized and quitting after only two weeks.
I wanted to make clear the price of a home for his revolver
after I'd read how disappointed I was.

But suppose we tried to place omnipotent hand into steaming
porcelain-white clouds,
the mystery of far-off novel quietly waiting in pencil . . .

I have wanted to kiss you I was born in
a little too hard a time in which myth was
going backward and forward faster and faster
until the last thing in the world
was dollars   I woke feeling indolent like
I was made of index cards reading
1980, MAKE IT FEEL, BRILLIANT FEATHERS
and other stuff   These days I can't
think of a single question I can live in
so let's buy a house there are so many things
about them I love   You must understand
I want to *ruin* prose   I write but all in all
I do very little I can't be embarrassed
because knowing is never going to disguise
my experience   It's got a futon in it because
I have no control over irony   Your email was
not a story I could find myself in it was
full of dogs and snow and you with your hair
all whipped about by the wind I think
this is how I would describe culture I think
this is how I would describe how I want to feel

How to draw houses. Always draw a red house whenever possible. Pretend it is your mother's house. Poplars in the foreground are not recommended. Yellow birch, however, are fine when drawn expertly— and in moderation. Birds of various feather are a pleasant addition. I always say, why settle for one or two when you can have several? Rain is an absolute no-no. Try erasing much of the house without causing its collapse—less is more, remember. Hedges can be iffy. These should be kept out front. Daylight is best suggested. (Didactic gestures, too, are extraneous.) As a general rule, you can achieve the right shading with a simple cross-hatch effect. Tar paper or clapboard? Choose accordingly. Refer to rule two in the case of dormers. A view from the west is particularly striking for sea-level dwellings. Choose fall: it's more poignant. You may draw from previous sketches for ideas.

A man stands before a mirror, pushing his teeth back into their sockets. Blood runs down his chin and bare chest into the porcelain basin below. When at last he is finished his gums are like very soft clay with shards of glass pushed into it. He then carefully rinses his mouth with alcohol. Out in the courtyard, he notices something gleaming among the compost. A pocket watch, its hands frozen at nine o'clock. He can hear that old blind woman down the block scolding her poor dog: "Bad girl! Bad girl!" He remembers that the diner is always quiet at this hour. He orders the soup on account of his teeth. Two tables over, Mr. Cunningham is annoying the waitress: "I seem to have misplaced my pocket watch." Outside, suspended high above the village, a street performer is doing a trapeze walk while reciting a poem to his dead mother. (Her presence for him, he sings, is like warm water being poured into his being.) But a stray dog ruins his composure, and he falls, bashing his teeth in. It is nine o'clock.

EVERY DAY IS IGNOBLE

The lamp was still burning when I awoke,
the sultry night air eloquent in the blinds.
The soft chair had become hard.
I got up and returned to my books.
We are found among our objects, each
as breakable as us.

•

Again, the day at my back.
Do I believe it? To lose this play
of real and unreal. No one ever tells us surrender
is hard work. Continually,
I sink into that essential meanness:
I will decide what is real.

•

No action or inertia can give us ourselves.
I listen: footsteps echo in the parking lot below,
only footsteps. The chair creaks
as I bend to my small thoughts.
Two points converge and beg order.
Should I lie close, N, when I come back to bed?

A picture is nothing
but little dots. What surprised me most
was how moved I was by that valley.
I still love this record.
Sure the sky has hardened. Just look at it.
Somehow I keep opening windows.

I know that loop.
It's one syllable getting pulled through the next.
Remember me losing my glove?
It looked so wounded there on the sidewalk
you were compelled to take a picture.
There was a word not being said
somewhere in the world
that was needing to be said.
I'm thinking that's significant.

The moon just hung there.
We thought it was supposed to do something.
To us, inside. It was a long time
before I spoke. I swear if that kid
keeps beating that goddamn drum.
The thaw-trickle coming down the parking lot

is really spilt milk.
The light says so.

Only some things are hidden.
Or everything is.
You can tear away at this life all you want.
In it, just three purple leaves. No, four.
We ended up with the same
hotel room again.
And aberrant pink
lacquer-cleaving my book.
Why am I the only mute thing in this place?
We landed smack in the street,
as if in a space made for us. We are
all of us groping through someone else's past.
Explain to me, just what is beauty.
I see mud and bermy snow.

A man finds the lawn has mown itself.
Listen. You'll find loping swags of guitar
and not much else.
It's okay to stay naked. History
reads itself aloud. I go back to bed in my clothes
like a cigarette
put back in its pack unsmoked.

That's bells you're hearing.
Or the last bits of joy
being shook out of the day, depends.
We exist between images. That we're forced

to wade through huge vats of poetry
each day suggests actual malice.
E.g., what's with all these birds
elatedly screaming their heads off?
E.g., is malice ever actual?

The nightmare is losing.
We accept that there are greater crimes
than remembering. We accept
that there are greater crimes than fucking
while our breakfast goes cold.
There is nothing I can ask this room.
I have exactly two hands.

The petticoats are coming, Mr. Beasley.
Delightful. This one was to help the guests from
their carriages, thus creating the diversion of
anchoring them in a kind of narrative, while the other
led the unwitting victims down the long, fog-strewn
path into nonsense. It was in this way the laureate
was able to carry out the plot for years.

There the massive snow impinged upon the landscape,
though winter's locutions had been sent packing, all
eighteen miles of lucite hair crashing to the shoulders of the road.
Nevertheless, the season remained a minor masterpiece, and
        embedded with moments of unscripted giddiness. A few kernels
of late-afternoon light would lay scattered on the incognizant ground,
        the archipelago of ideas they
might have illumined unfortunately stored away in the brain until
        spring.
At times, life was expected to be a sharp admixture of gnarled
        ambition and an old-fashioned
standard-issue negligence, which it is, though at times
the watermark of reckoning tended to give one away.
Building secret escape routes into each decision one made was an
        acceptable, even
encouraged practice amongst our kind.

So these frayed intentions did little to quell the general, all-around
frustration of the bas relief that is those years, is that what you're
    saying?
Yes and no. You see, we are coming up on a rampart in our day.
Suddenly a cure for solitude is upon us,
and before you know it, the lesson'll be finished off in just a few bites,
altering the synaptic weight forever. But we are condemned to repeal it,
caught as we are in emoting all up in each other's personal space.

Well, good luck anyway, Fireplaces. I'll be seeing you.

Of course I can't expect intoxicating anus like the other guys,
hundreds of guys washing and dressing in flower bed.
In future I shan't allow bonnet to resemble one another.
Slowly, he lowered his breeches. Years passed.

I began to think the whole thing made me think of fiercely thrilling
time when dude peered warily into 45th annual hoo-ha.
Everything around here I tried to breathe
in a sort of panic, except he was visited by beaklike nose
primly fussing over small rocket. I was a corpse by then.

Supper was clarinet with fried onions. Only thing missing was
Osbert trying to look photogenic, picking at bonhomie.
A thousand of hours later, silence was so excruciating,
the smell more and more intense as she approached the barn,
sun gliding past approximately nineteen years ago.

I shall in due time let go these umbrella.
That's all I meant by it. This wavering will
die! die! die! with invigorating shampoo at top speed.

Some poets like the bitter taste. Why do I keep writing?
I've created many blurry, murky, dark and mediocre embraces.
I enjoy chugging 'em down, albeit in limited measure.

Christmas loaf had only to look impassive and of most
agreeable aspect, which I found hard to believe.
Finger pointed at prostrate body. He wanted it.

Was quite high one night with boy, six dollars' worth of
madness in his eyes, and quite predisposed toward strange behavior.
The sphinx had an art house feel to it: 'twas our fate.
I had not foreseen low-hanging bell, however, as
sea was smacking up against it with dear demolished wisdom.

Today, at approximately 4 p.m., the sky perished.

It is with God now.

If any one of us could say what it is that is left in its place, could
    describe

to his fellow men just what it is we see now

when we look up, we surely would.

But since none of us can, we say nothing.

Somehow this silence seems to communicate everything we need
    to say.

All of us the world over have agreed, consequently,

to the banishment of all language.

This agreement, it must be said,

was arrived at in total silence, without the exchange

of a single word, written or verbal, without

a single sign. It came hurtling instantaneously into our heads

with such explosive force that it has incapacitated

us all. This is to tell you that.

Our hopes are that this message oscillates safely within you.

Streetboy, please   What I *need* is a thousand tiny

kinfolk to point me toward the nougaty epi-

center of mine own heart   I hear there's a trailer

park there where my tiny electronic voice lives

I hear there's a star that waters your ugly

I hear contentment seeping from a too-small chair

I am stepping into one pantleg then another

and another and another and another and another

I am thinking there's a mesmerism furloughed

in this possum not going away and *what is this*

diagram coming out of my face trying to mean?

We could be so far away from absolutely nothing

and unending it is like that sometimes nowhere

near this place where a string is vibrating

unimaginably inside our moment inside our

widening us-ness   A spindly clairaudience

a soiled rainbow a burst of chickens a diminutive

Buddha a rookie seawall—all of it ours   Hours

If I am given to understand splendid stupidity I can well imagine

false or nonsense as I do not know anything.

It cannot be escaped, the mystery thus solved and to be used

in the construction of my sandwich, my Band-Aid

accumulating words, restaurants, marine species, and bebop.

There you will find large silver stripe, broken only by

very fine sephirah. The buzzer was missing.

Then came a string of days so heavy no man could lift them,

a few snowflakes penetrating the gentleman's greatcoat,

this little parlor game causing great snatches of laughter from

punchbowl, which would shudder through me from time to time,

as previously noted. No, that is an exaggeration:

change is not possible when body is floating ukulele.

On the eve of our entrance into the next form, I took a train to Dessau with Mosbey and Bloch. Though I have repeated it several times since childhood, I have always retained the novelty of this trip from even my earliest years. Thus I was able to partake in the excitement which consumed my two friends. Often, alone, I have made the voyage by day on some pretext or other for a visit with Clara, whom I first met upon leaving a small shop while on a trip there with mother some months prior. But this was my first by night, which may account for something very odd that befell us upon entering the street in which Clara lived. At least that is all I can think to explain it. It seems someone had removed all the addresses from the tenement houses, or they were not discernable at any rate. But that was not the principle problem. Nothing was at all familiar; there were none of the usual landmarks to guide my way. And yet I was somehow sure this was the correct neighborhood, though the street was not run athwart with the usual night-faring types. Perhaps the fog and increasing chill had some bearing here. We wandered for hours before coming upon the place, the three of us weary and irritable. The rooming house was even more decrepit and disreputable-looking than I'd remembered it. An elderly man in a shabby suit stood eyeing us from the doorway. "May I help you?" he said politely. "Help us?" I demanded, "Who are you?" "I"—he bowed—"am the concierge." I could see that he was missing several teeth. "Concierge? Here?" He gestured for us to enter. "Please," he waved us toward a threadbare divan crammed into a narrow space under the stairs. "I shall see if the lady wishes any company this evening," he said, and disappeared behind a door, only to reemerge barely a moment later: "I'm sorry, but the lady is ill." "What's the meaning of this?" I cried, pushing past the old man and swinging wide the door. Beyond was an enormous, lavishly decorated room as in a royal palace. Two chambermaids immediately leapt to their feet and set about cleaning and straightening, though the room did not seem to warrant it. The women were rapt in conversation, gesticulating to one another, yet not a sound sprang from their lips. It then occurred to me with some displeasure that I had been sep-arated into two distinct, rather flimsy halves, Mosbey holding onto one, Bloch the other . . .

I'm so glad you came that day, that day a house

fell down inside my gut   I could've blotted out

the sky, blotted out all faces with the bloodhands

In my head a thousand pounds of glass

was being crushed and now there is never any

coming back from that day I shut out the eyes,

that day I fucked the light with the bloodhands

So let's reach into our mouths and rip out all the

shadows   Let's go out into the street and knock down

all the shadows   Let's collect all the little hammers

and see how they sound when we toss them into

the void   In this moment we are sprawled out betwixt our

proximal dimensions with our faces all screwed up

into what   It's from here the gods of 5:30 Pacific Standard

Time tell of your colors, they tell me you are really two

thousand seagulls, they tell of the seizures inside the grace

and of the saga of my alarm heart buried,

buried under the steps for climbing up into your song

HATSKOK

Nothing is going to happen to you
Simply by writing a letter and getting on a plane.
There's delirium and there's
The world and I seem to be talking about
The thing that will open up
The plausible. In a parking lot
I felt the world would be a better place if
I were to watch it disappear. What I
Remember is we walked for blocks
And blocks and we were like
An elegant sentence. Language
Is what happens to you. You have to choose
A heart made of wood
And money to make it all work.
But it doesn't work. And I am
A beautiful fragment and it's okay.

A number of the poems in this collection originally appeared in the following publications, sometimes in slightly different form: *BlazeVox, Display, Kindling, NightBlock, Past Simple, Tallow Eider Quarterly, Thieves Jargon, Trnsfr, Unlikely Stories, Untoward, Vinyl*, and in the chapbook *Status Area* (Varmint Armature, 2011).

———

First and foremost, I'd like to thank Jen Tynes for generously accepting this collection for publication. Thanks to Paul Maliszewski and Kath Marty for their steadfast friendship over the years; to Katherine Sullivan for her longstanding support, friendship, and, as one of the first readers of this manuscript, for offering invaluable feedback and encouragement; and to Roxane Gay, for giving me my start in book design.

I'd also like to thank all the poets, writers, editors, publishers, designers, artists, and others who have in one way or another encouraged me, inspired me, or supported my work over the past decade and more (whether or not they knew it), or who have simply been a pleasure to know: James Tadd Adcox; Eric Amling; Andrew Bailey; Stephanie Barber; Jody Bates; Ken Bauman; Jessica Berger; Peter Berghoef; Joshua Bohnsack; Mel Bosworth; Ryan W. Bradley; Charles Brock, Torrey Sharp, and everyone at Faceout Studio; Melissa Broder; Paul Buckley; Marty Cain; Mairead Case; Sarah Clark; John Colasacco; Shanna Compton; Robert Andy Coombs; Dennis Cooper;

David Cope; Jacob Covey; Christy Crutchfield; Chase Dearinger, Corey Mingura, and everyone at *Arcadia*; Joseph Demes; the Division Avenue Arts Collective; Stephen Dixon; Zach Dodson; Thom Donovan; Brandon Downing; Tim Earley; WYCE's *Electric Poetry*; Elizabeth Ellen; Catherine Eves; Ashley Farmer; Archie Ferguson; Tim Fisher; Kyle Flak; Molly Gaudry; Marco Giovenale; Amanda Goldblatt; Sarah Gorham, Danika Isdahl, and everyone at Sarabande Books; Joseph Grantham; Jon Gray; everyone at the Great Lakes Commonwealth of Letters; Ruth Greenstein, Casey Hannan; Will Hubbard; Naomi Huffman; Abi Humber, Amanda Leigh Lichtenstein, and everyone at 826CHI; Michael Ingold; Jac Jemc; Peter Jurmu; W. Todd Kaneko; Anton Khodakovsky; Catherine Lacey; Dorothea Lasky; Lynn Melnick; Mark Melnick; Kasey Mohammad; Lara Mimosa Montes; Dolan Morgan; Daniela Olszewska; Joe Pan; Schyler Perkins; Michael Pfleghaar; Kristen Radtke; Katie Raissian; Ryan Ridge; Joseph Riipi; Adam Robinson; Kathleen Rooney; Shya Scanlon; Jenn Schaub; Michael J. Seidlinger; M. Bartley Seigel; Michael Sikkema; Amber Sparks; The Sparrows Coffee & Tea & Newsstand; Troy Stouten; Michael Stutz; Tim Taranto; Jason Teal; J.A. Tyler; Dan Wagstaff; Brandi Wells; the members of the West Michigan Writers' Workshop in the early aughts; George Wietor; Ola Wihlke; Marco Seiryu Wilkinson; Tom Williams; Rebecca Wolff; and Mike Young. Apologies to anyone I've forgotten.

And finally, deepest gratitude to my partner, Nicholas Coppernoll, for your ceaseless love, and the awesome example of your boundless thoughtfulness, fortitude, and exuberance. Thanks, also, to my parents Tom and Roxanne, and to my siblings Elle, David, Brian, and Tracy.

ALBAN FISCHER is the founding editor of *Trnsfr* and Trnsfr Books. He has designed over 350 books, and worked with more than sixty organizations, including 826CHI, Alice James Books, *The Believer*, Bellevue Literary Press, Coffee House Press, Columbia University Press, Faceout Studio, Open Letter Books, Turtle Point Press, and Verso. His work has been included in the AUPresses Book, Jacket, and Journal Show, selected for AIGA and Design Observer's 50 Books / 50 Covers, and has been recognized by The Book Cover Archive, *The Casual Optimist*, and *Spine* Magazine. He lives in Grand Rapids, Michigan, where he serves as Graphic Designer for YesYes Books and Art Director of Sarabande Books. His work can be found online at albanfischerdesign.com.